Contents

Emergency vehicle safety
Cars, trucks, boats and motorbikes are powerful
machines. They can be very dangerous. Always have an
adult with you when you look at emergency vehicles.
Do not stand behind vehicles. Never touch vehicles.

first book of
emergency
vehicles

Isabel Thomas

For Harry, Joey and Oscar

Published 2014 by
A&C Black
An imprint of Bloomsbury Publishing Plc
50 Bedford Square, London, WC1B 3DP

www.bloomsbury.com

ISBN 978-1-4081-9457-7

This book is produced using paper that is made from wood
grown in managed, sustainable forests. It is natural, renewable
and recyclable. The logging and manufacturing processes
conform to the environmental regulations of the country of origin.

Printed in China by C&C.

10 9 8 7 6 5 4 3 2 1

Emergency vehicles

Emergency vehicles help people in need. They rush to emergencies as quickly as possible, carrying useful equipment. Look out for the flashing lights of police cars and motorbikes. Listen for the wail of ambulance and fire engine sirens.

You can find emergency vehicles on and off the road. You can spot them in the air and on water. This book will help you to name all the different types of emergency vehicles.

At the back of this book is a Spotter's Guide to help you remember the emergency vehicles you see. Tick them off as you spot them. You can also find out the meaning of some useful words here.

Turn the page to find out all about emergency vehicles!

Police helicopter

The police use helicopters to find missing people, chase criminals, and guide police officers on the ground. A helicopter can search a huge area in minutes.

Special cameras spot warm things like people and cars – even if they are hiding in the dark!

Rotor

Tail rotor

Thermal imaging camera

Cockpit

Bright searchlight

Landing skids

Police helicopters also help with rescue missions.

Fire engine

Most fire engines have water tanks, long hoses, and ladders. They can pump water to fight fires, and help to rescue people trapped in burning buildings.

Tanks full of water are very heavy. Fire engines need to be powerful.

Ladders

Water cannon

Tool lockers

Big cab to carry crew

When the water in the tank runs out, the fire engine pumps water from a river, tanker truck, or fire hydrant.

Ambulance

Ambulances speed sick and injured people to hospital. They travel very fast in an emergency. They carry life-saving equipment to treat patients.

A loud siren warns other vehicles to clear the road.

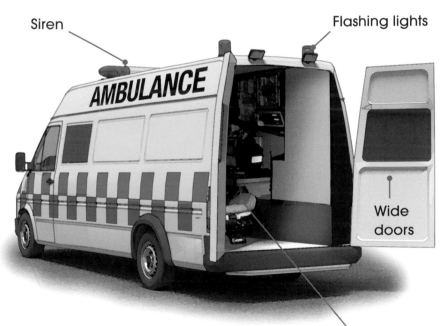

Siren

Flashing lights

Wide doors

Folding stretcher

Most ambulances have a crew of two. One person drives, while the other looks after patients on the way to hospital.

Mountain rescue vehicle

Tough vehicles help with search and rescue missions in areas without roads. They rescue people who get into trouble on mountainsides, forests, and moors.

The rescue vehicle can pull itself out of mud or snow using the winch. It can also rescue other vehicles that are stuck.

Flashing lights

Roof rack

Emergency equipment

Winch

Body high off ground

Tyres grip rough ground

Airport rescue and firefighting vehicle

Fire engines like this work at airports. They can speed to a burning aircraft in minutes. The crew use controls to fight fires from inside the cab.

The crew can also fight fires by hand, using long hoses.

Tool lockers

Huge water tank

Large wheels

The long arm rises up to spray foam over an aeroplane.

Long arm

Water cannon (monitor)

Cab

Camera helps the crew to find the hottest parts of a fire

In one minute, the cannons spray enough foam to fill 75 bathtubs.

Police car

Police cars transport police officers and criminals. They search for missing people. They patrol roads to warn traffic not to drive too fast. They race to help at accidents and emergencies.

Police drivers are trained to drive fast safely.

A two-way radio keeps police officers in touch with other police cars, helicopters, and base.

Radio aerial

Police markings

Flashing lights

Bull bars

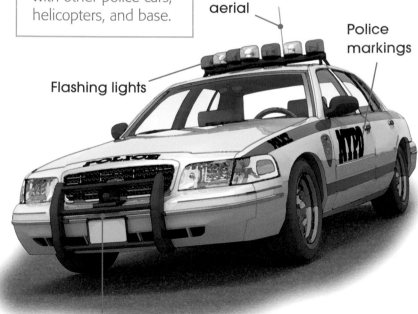

Air ambulance

Flying ambulances get people to hospital very quickly. They can reach places that are difficult to get to by road. Helicopters can land almost anywhere.

The tail rotor is covered, so people can walk around the helicopter safely.

Tail rotor

Cabin with room for paramedic, passenger, and patient on stretcher

Bubble windscreen gives the pilot a good view

Large sliding door

Stretchers can be loaded through large doors at the sides and back.

Ladder engine

Some fire engines carry extra-long ladders, or folding arms with platforms on top. They can spray water on fires from above, and rescue people from tall buildings.

Water is pumped up to a nozzle at the top of the ladder.

Nozzle

Extending ladder

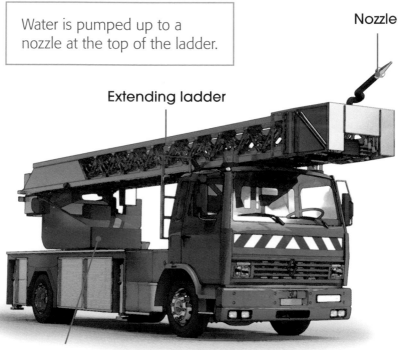

Turntable

The turntable swivels to point the ladder in any direction.

Offshore lifeboat

Lifeboats rescue people who are in trouble at sea. This large lifeboat can go out in stormy weather and travel through huge, crashing waves.

If a wave knocks it over, the lifeboat rolls itself the right way up again.

More than 120 survivors can squeeze on board.

Radar

Small inflatable lifeboat for shallow water

Wheelhouse

Wipers

Hull

Police personal transporter

Segways and scooters let police officers zip around shopping centres, airports, and stations. Electric motors make them smooth and quiet.

This Segway helps police patrol a large area three times faster than by foot.

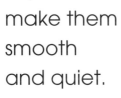

The rider moves by leaning the way they want to go.

Bag for equipment

Fireboat

Fireboats help burning ships and boats. They pump water straight from the sea, and squirt it through water cannons. Look out for fireboats spraying water at special events.

The cannons can spray water more than twice as far as a hose.

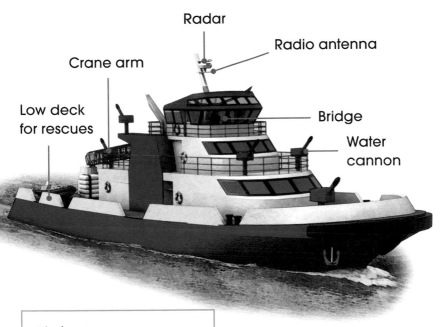

Radar

Radio antenna

Crane arm

Low deck for rescues

Bridge

Water cannon

Fireboats can pump seawater for fire engines to use on land.

Search and rescue helicopter

Helicopters can take off and land without runways. They can hover in one spot.

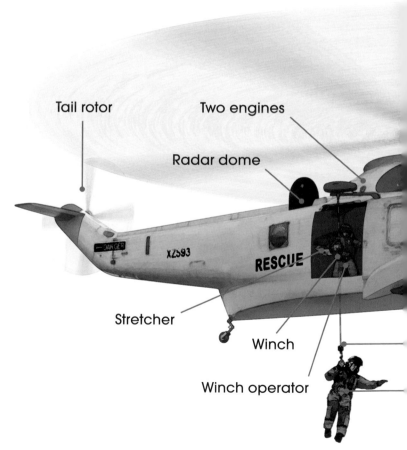

Tail rotor

Two engines

Radar dome

XZ593

RESCUE

Stretcher

Winch

Winch operator

This makes them great for rescue missions in places without roads.

The crew uses a cable and winch to lift survivors on board.

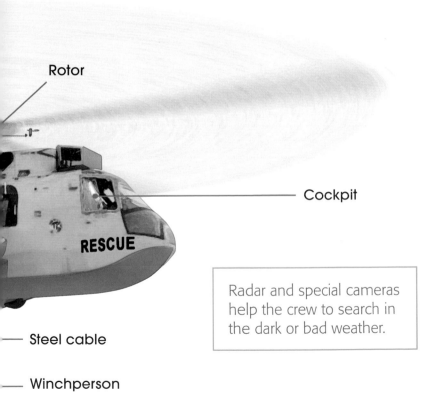

Rotor

Cockpit

RESCUE

Radar and special cameras help the crew to search in the dark or bad weather.

Steel cable

Winchperson

Personal watercraft

Lifeguards use personal watercraft with rescue sleds. They can reach struggling swimmers quickly, and tow them back to shore.

Personal watercraft work in shallow water. They can be parked on the sand.

In some countries, personal watercraft patrol the sea looking for sharks.

Seat

Steering column

Rescue sled

Engine

Police van

Police forces use vans to transport prisoners and suspects safely. Vans can also carry a large group of police officers to an emergency.

Some police vans have special areas for police dogs.

Dark windows   Flashing lights   Windscreen shield

A barrier separates prisoners and police officers.

Firefighting aeroplane

This aeroplane fights wildfires. It scoops up water by swooping across a lake, river, or sea. The pilot drops the water on the fire and flies off to fill the tank again.

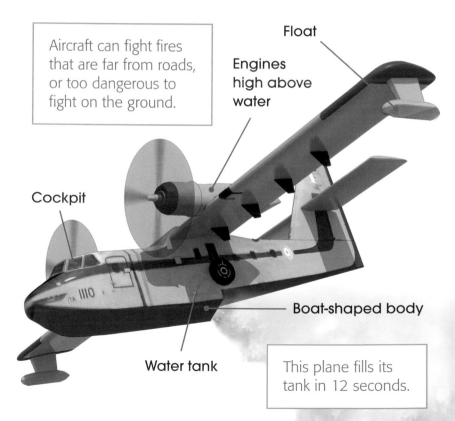

Aircraft can fight fires that are far from roads, or too dangerous to fight on the ground.

Float

Engines high above water

Cockpit

Boat-shaped body

Water tank

This plane fills its tank in 12 seconds.

Emergency bicycle

Police and paramedics speed through busy cities on bicycles. They can dodge traffic, ride up and down steps, cut through alleyways, and cycle into buildings.

Emergency services use tough mountain bikes.

Bicycles often beat police cars and ambulances to emergencies.

Helmet

Radio

Reflective clothes

Siren

Panniers carry life-saving kit

Puncture-proof tyres

Amphibious rescue vehicle

Amphibious vehicles come to the rescue when water is too shallow for lifeboats, but too deep for rescue trucks. They can drive from land straight into water.

The front unit can tow a crane to pull vehicles out of the water.

Front unit carries six crew

Tracks spread the truck's weight.

Tracks

Rear unit can carry 12 rescued people

Recovery truck

Recovery trucks are called out when a car, truck, or bus breaks down. They help to clear roads after accidents.

The biggest recovery trucks can tow huge lorries and buses.

Winch

Flashing lights

Bright markings warn other vehicles to stay clear

Recovery trucks carry tools to mend broken vehicles. They tow away vehicles that can't be fixed.

Police boat

Police forces use boats to patrol rivers, ports, and coasts. Boats like this are called launches.

Radar

Satellite communications help the crew keep in touch with land.

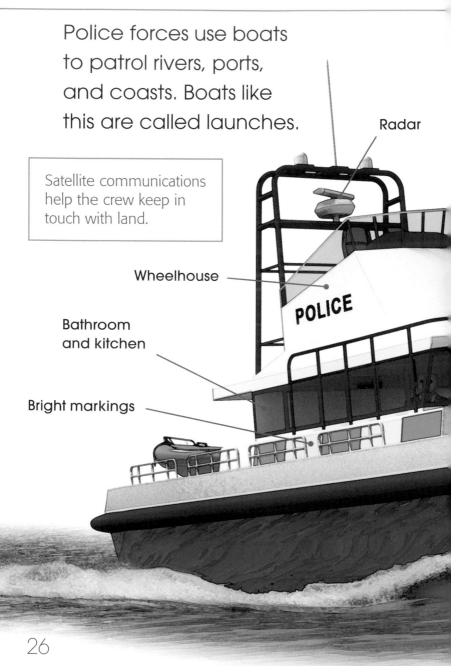

Wheelhouse

Bathroom and kitchen

Bright markings

POLICE

They have speedy engines, and equipment to help with searches and rescues.

This boat can drive up a beach.

Searchlight

Night vision cameras help police to work in bad weather, or in the dark.

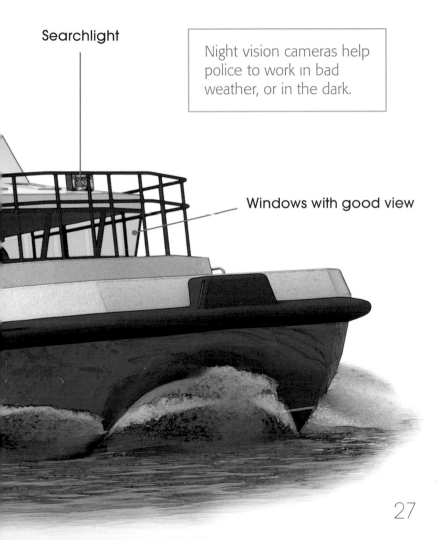

Windows with good view

Underwater rescue submersible

This small craft goes on dangerous rescue missions deep underwater. It lands on top of damaged submarines. Survivors crawl in through the rescue hatch.

The submersible dives by letting water into its huge tanks.

The grabber arm cuts through wreckage, and moves things out of the way.

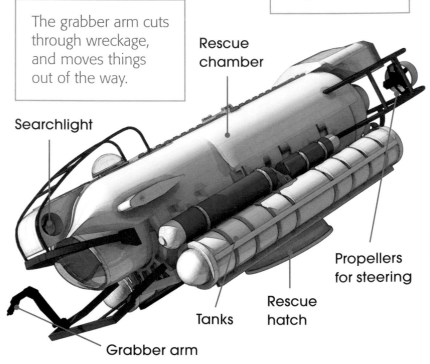

Rescue chamber

Searchlight

Propellers for steering

Tanks

Rescue hatch

Grabber arm

Inshore rescue boat

Small, inflatable lifeboats can be launched from a beach or a larger boat. They rescue people from shallow water, caves, and other places where big lifeboats can't go.

This inshore lifeboat is light enough for two people to carry into the water.

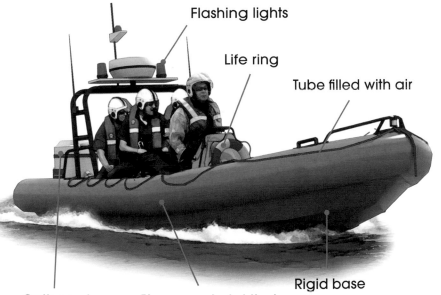

Flashing lights

Life ring

Tube filled with air

Rigid base

Outboard engine

Strong material that is like rubber

Fire rescue support unit

Fire rescue vehicles help in emergencies such as floods, traffic accidents, and earthquakes. They carry tools and equipment to help firefighters rescue people.

This vehicle can work with a water tanker truck to put out fires.

Hoses

Lockers for tools and protective gear

Surf rescue quad bike

Lifeguards use quad bikes to get around beaches quickly. Light frames and chunky tyres help the bikes to travel across sand.

Quad bikes are much smaller than trucks, so they can be used on busy beaches.

The driver can see all around.

Rack to carry equipment

Headlight

Chunky tyres

Firefighting helicopter

These helicopters fight fires from the sky. Some have water tanks on board.

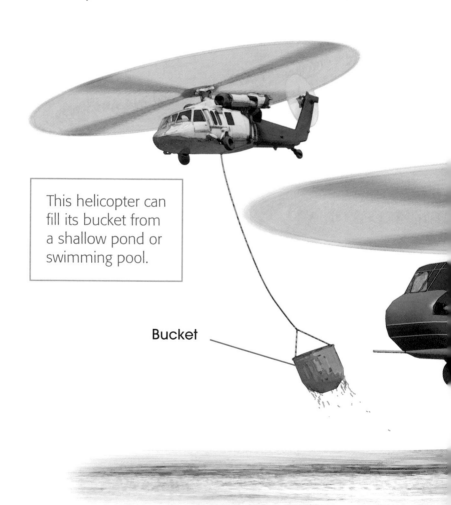

This helicopter can fill its bucket from a shallow pond or swimming pool.

Bucket

Others carry huge buckets. The
pilot hovers over the fire and
presses a button to drop the water.

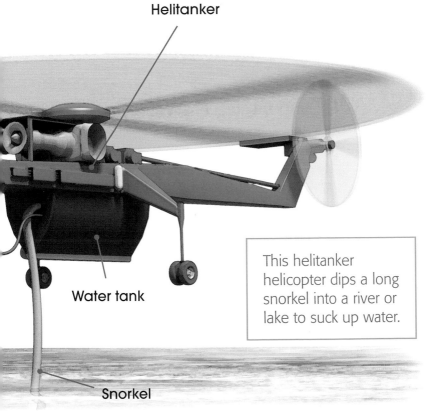

Helitanker

Water tank

Snorkel

This helitanker
helicopter dips a long
snorkel into a river or
lake to suck up water.

Flying Doctor

In Australia, some people live very far from a hospital. Aeroplane ambulances rescue sick and injured patients. They can travel further and faster than helicopters.

The aeroplanes are like flying hospital wards. There are beds and equipment to keep patients alive.

Engine

Cabin with room for patients on stretchers

The Royal Flying Doctor Service has more than 60 aircraft.

Propeller

Coastguard boat

This strong and speedy boat does many different jobs. Coastguards help at emergencies near the coast. They carry out rescue missions and make sure people obey the law at sea.

A bumper lets the boat stop next to other boats without being damaged.

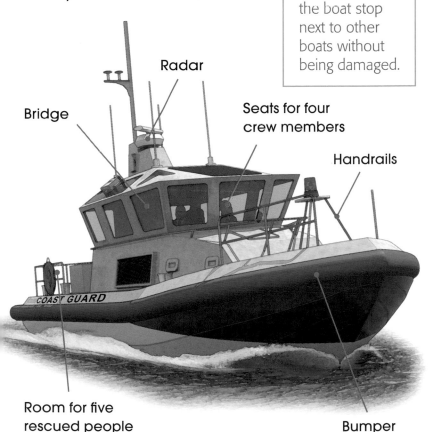

Radar

Bridge

Seats for four crew members

Handrails

COAST GUARD

Room for five rescued people

Bumper

Fire train

Fires inside railway tunnels are very dangerous. In some countries, special fire trains speed to the rescue.

Rescue wagon

This fire train has three wagons. One carries a huge water tank.

Tank wagon

Water cannon

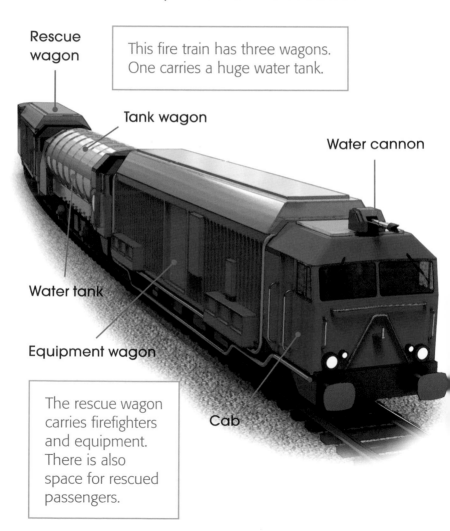

Water tank

Equipment wagon

The rescue wagon carries firefighters and equipment. There is also space for rescued passengers.

Cab

Armoured police truck

Highly trained police teams rush to the most difficult and dangerous emergencies. Armoured trucks keep the teams and their gear safe.

Large police trucks act as control centres during disasters.

Small windows

Sloping windscreen

Black paint

Bulletproof glass

Radiator guard

Steel walls, floor, roof, and doors

Tough tyres

Emergency motorcycle

Police, fire, and paramedic motorbikes weave through crowded streets, cut through alleyways, and zoom up and down steps.

Police motorbike

Flashing light

Bright patterns

POLICE

Paramedic motorbikes carry life-saving equipment and medicine.

Fire motorbikes carry enough water and foam to fight small fires.

Flashing lights

Panniers full of equipment

Hose reel

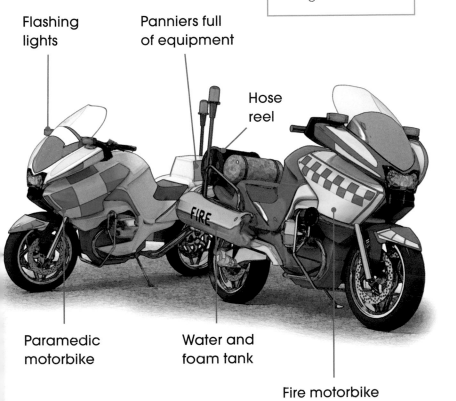

Paramedic motorbike

Water and foam tank

Fire motorbike

Off-road fire truck

This tough truck fights fires in the countryside. Large, tough tyres help it drive over bumpy ground, up steep hillsides, and across deep rivers.

Water tank

Chunky tyres

The truck sprays water and foam at huge fires as it drives.

Storage lockers with equipment for fighting fires and rescuing animals

Useful words

crew the group of people that work on an emergency vehicle

engine a machine that burns fuel to make a vehicle go

fire hydrant a place where a fire engine can get water from underground pipes

monitor another name for a water cannon

nozzle the spout at the end of a hose

paramedic a person who is trained to give emergency medical help

patrol travel around an area to keep watch over it

radar a system that uses radio waves to detect objects on or above water

rotor the spinning blades that lift a helicopter into the air

suspension springs and shock absorbers that stop a vehicle ride from being too bumpy

two-way radio a radio set used to talk to someone else

winch a machine that lets out and pulls in a long cable

Spotter's guide

How many of these emergency
vehicles have you seen?
Tick them when you spot them.

☐ Police
helicopter
page 6

☐ Fire engine
page 7

☐ Ambulance
page 8

☐ Mountain
rescue vehicle
page 9

Airport rescue and firefighting vehicle
page 10

Police car
page 12

Air ambulance
page 13

Ladder engine
page 14

Offshore lifeboat
page 15

Police personal transporter
page 16

☐ Amphibious
rescue vehicle
page 24

☐ Recovery truck
page 25

☐ Police boat
page 26

☐ Underwater rescue
submersible
page 28

☐ Inshore rescue
boat
page 29

☐ Fire rescue
support unit
page 30

Surf rescue
quad bike

Firefighting
helicopter

Flying Doctor

Coastguard
boat

Fire train

Armoured
police truck

Emergency
motorcycle
page 38

Off-road fire
truck
page 40

Find out more

If you would like to find out more about emergency vehicles, you could visit a transport museum. These websites are a good place to start.

Fire And Police Museum Sheffield
www.firepolicemuseum.org.uk

London Fire Brigade Museum
www.london-fire.gov.uk/OurMuseum.asp

National Maritime Museum Cornwall
www.nmmc.co.uk/